If the world is round, then why is the ground flat?

World Book
answers YOUR questions
- about -
Science

WORLD
BOOK

www.worldbook.com

The questions in this book came from curious kids just like you who want to make sense of the world. They wrote to us at World Book with nothing but a question and a dream that the question they've agonized over would finally be answered.

Some questions made us laugh. Others made us cry. And a few made us question absolutely everything we've ever known. No matter the responses they induced, all the questions were good questions.

There isn't a strict rule for what makes a question good. But asking any question means that you want to learn and to understand. And both of those things are very good.

Adults are always asking, "What did you learn at school today?" Instead, we think they should be asking, **"Did you ask a good question today?"**

Is there anything inside the **core** of Earth?

Yes.

But as much as we want it to be true, Earth does not have a delicious candy center. Instead, the core is made up of other, less-delicious things. The center has iron, nickel, sulfur, oxygen, silicon, and possibly smaller amounts of lighter elements. But, we are sorry to say, no caramel.

Why is the sky blue?

Blue is the sky's favorite color.

No, we're just kidding. We wish it was that simple. Sunlight is made up of light waves of different lengths. As these waves travel from the sun to Earth, they can be interrupted and scattered by particles in the air. We can see this scattering with our own eyes, and it looks like a color. Short, blue light waves are easily scattered by such tiny particles as the gas molecules that fill our atmosphere, making the sky look blue.

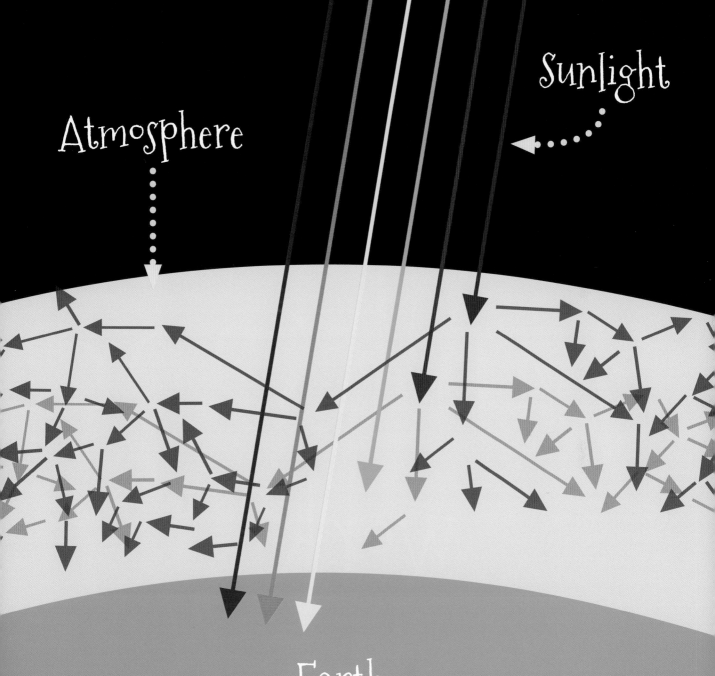

How does quicksand work?

13

Not well on a deadline.

Quicksand is a soft mass of wet sand that yields easily to pressure. It likes to work in places you wouldn't typically think were offices, like on the bottoms of streams and on sand flats along seacoasts. It doesn't work well under pressure because it behaves a lot like a fluid. Water flowing through the grains of sand forces them apart and prevents them from settling. In this condition, the sand loses its firmness and cannot support heavy weight.

Save the Coastline

15

Do you know how a huge tree comes from a tiny seed?

We do! And we have a **tree**mendous answer. First, the seed comes from a parent tree. Then it waits. And waits. And waits. Until water, air, and sunshine help the seed *germinate,* or begin to grow. The part of the seed that becomes the trunk points upward toward the sunlight. The itty-bitty seed absorbs water, and the root *bursts* through the seed's shell. The food in the seed helps the tree grow. The tree is ready to begin its long **leaf** as a tree.

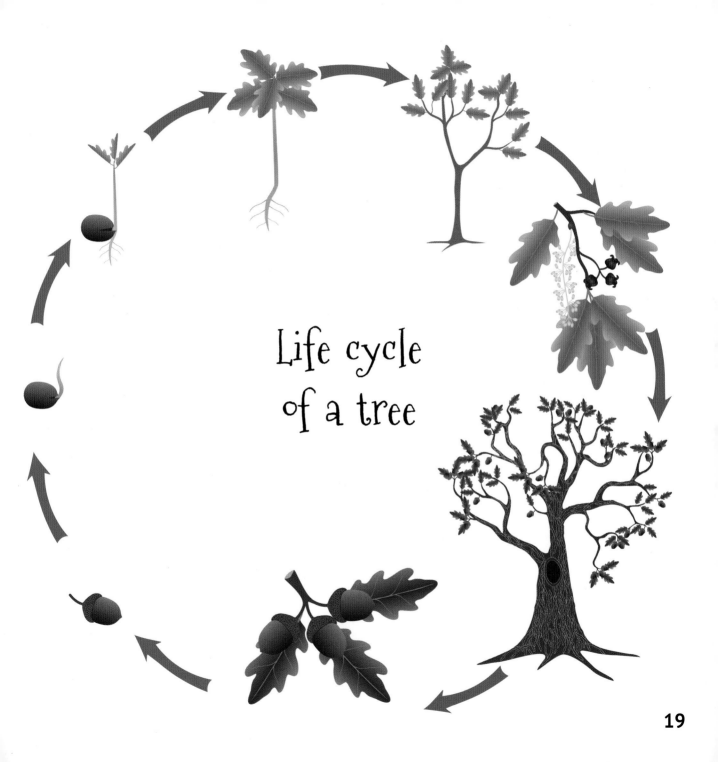

Life cycle
of a tree

If the world is round, then why is the ground flat?

(Still not chocolate.)

It might seem
like the ground is flat,
but it is actually curved.

But it's so, so slight that we don't notice it. Try

imagining it like this. If a cat and a bug were both

standing on a beach ball, the cat would be big

enough to know it's standing on a round surface.

But the beach ball would be so big to the bug,

it would feel like it was standing on a

flat surface. Humans are the

itty-bitty bug in this case.

23

Why does popcorn pop?

It can't wait to be smothered in butter.

But before it's soaked in salty goodness, some science is involved. When the water inside a kernel gets hot, it turns into steam. As the steam gets more and more steamy, the pressure inside the kernel gets stronger and stronger. Soon, the pressure causes the kernel to **POP**! The cooled starch in the kernel hardens into the fluffy shape of popcorn that is ready to eat. *Now* you can soak it in butter.

How are rainbows

formed?

By pots of gold landing on the ground, of course.

When that fails, there's science. A rainbow appears when raindrops are illuminated by sunlight. That means a rainbow cannot appear in a part of the sky where there isn't any rain. Did you know that no two people ever see the same rainbow? You are at the center of the rainbow you see. A person standing next to you would be at the center of a different rainbow. A different set of raindrops forms each rainbow.

How do flowers get their color?

Hint:

From tiny painters.

They use blades of grass for brushes and berries for colors. But, when they have too many flowers to get to, the flowers' genes help. Genes are the parts of cells that determine which traits living things will get from their parents. So the color of the flower is decided long before it's born. It is very good to be a bright-colored flower.

Vibrant colors attract insects and bees, which help carry pollen from one flower to another. Then the flower plants can reproduce and make more bright flowers.

Does global warming mean it'll be summer all the time?

We wish.

Unfortunately, the reality of climate change is a lot less fun than endless summertime. It affects cold temperatures and extreme weather, too—think air-so-cold-you-can't-go-outside, floods-and-tornadoes-and-storms, droughts-that-make-it-hard-for-animals-to-live types of weather.

What is the sun made of?

While the sun might look like it's made of cheesy dust, that isn't the case.

The sun is made up mostly of atoms of hydrogen (the stuff that makes water). The second-most plentiful element is helium (the stuff that makes balloons float). There are also atoms of oxygen, carbon, neon, nitrogen, magnesium, iron, and silicon. The inside of the sun is mostly plasma, a super-hot gas.

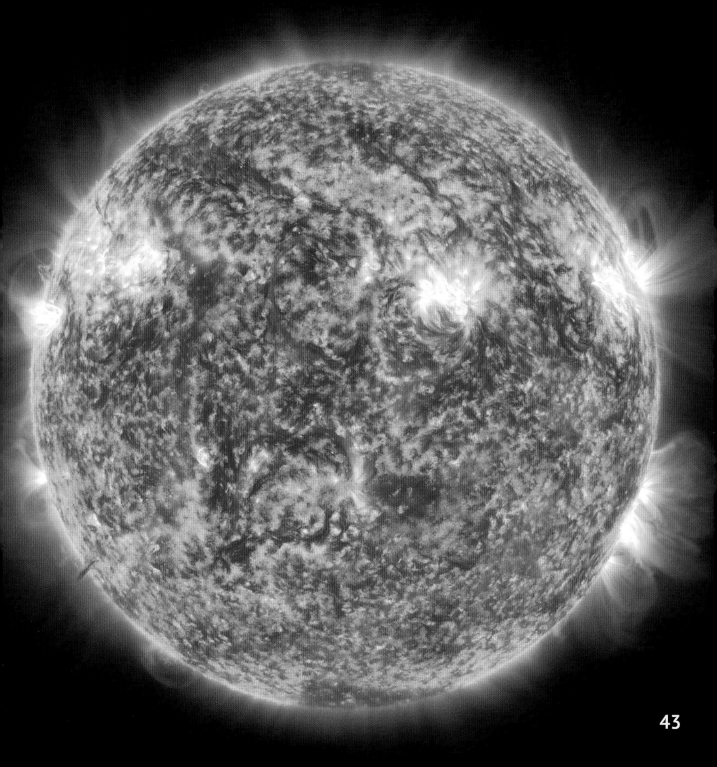

43

How do balloons float?

Magic.

But, if you forget to say "Abracadabra," there are other options. A balloon is a bag or envelope filled with heated air or a light gas. A balloon floats when the heated air or gas inside is lighter than the surrounding air.

Why does the moon follow my car as we drive?

It wants to join you on your trip!

It hopes you're heading somewhere warm. Just kidding. It might look like the moon is traveling along with you as you drive, but it's staying right in place. Objects that are really close to the car—like road signs and trees—go whirring past. Objects a little farther away—like buildings in the distance—move a bit slower across the window. The moon is just so, so far away that it looks as though it's going everywhere with you.

Why do some trees lose their leaves in fall?

To save water.

A deciduous tree sheds its leaves once a year. In northern regions, that usually happens in autumn. After the leaves fall off, the twigs and branches stay bare all winter. Scientists think that losing leaves helps some trees to conserve water in the winter. They think that because they're smart scientists. And because water normally passes into the air from tree leaves. That process is called transpiration.

What
do clouds
feel like?

Have you ever petted a bunny?

Or squished a really fluffy pillow? Or felt the puffy wisps of cotton candy? Well, good for you, but clouds feel nothing like that. Clouds are made of teeny, tiny drops of water that have evaporated from the earth into the sky. So clouds just feel... wet. Sometimes those water droplets freeze in the cold air. Those clouds would feel icy and cold.

Leave me out of this, please!

Why are there seasons?

To spice up bland chicken.

But you're probably talking about weather seasons, not food season**ings**. Earth's axis is not straight up and down—it's tilted. This tilt and the Earth's motion around the sun combine to cause the seasons.

In January, the northern half of Earth is pointed away from the sun, so the north experiences winter. At the same time, Earth's southern half is tilted towards the sun. That's when the south experiences summer.

January

What would happen if there was no gravity?

A lot.
And it wouldn't be good.

Gravity holds together the sun and keeps the planets in their orbits around the sun. Gravity also keeps you on the ground. And, while it might seem fun to float around like you're in a gigantic pool, we need gravity. We couldn't live without it.

Why does lightning always have straight lines, not curvy lines like a circle?

Simple answer: it doesn't.

Lightning appears in many different ways. One of these ways is as a circle. It is called ball lightning. It appears as a glowing, fiery ball that floats for a few seconds before disappearing. It is uncommon and can even occur indoors! Ball lightning can be red, yellow, or orange in color.

71

Why does the sun rise at different times?

Because sometimes it wants cereal for breakfast.

And other times it wants pancakes, sausage, bacon, and eggs. Just kidding! It eats a smoothie every morning, regardless of when it wakes up. The sun rises at different times because the tilt of Earth's axis causes first one pole to slant toward the sun and then the other as the planet orbits the sun. Together, these factors determine if your day has a lot of sunlight or a little.

Why don't people fall off of rollercoasters when they go upside down?

We can thank science for that one.

Roller coasters aren't all just fun and games—
it takes some serious brainiacs to *engineer* a
safe rollercoaster. Engineers use principles of
science to build structures, machines, and—
yep—even roller coasters. The principle at
work when a rollercoaster goes upside down
is called *centrifugal* force, which keeps you in
your seat as you make a loop-di-loop. Try filling
a bucket with water and waving it in a circle
above your head. If you move quickly enough,
not a drop of water will spill out. Same force.

How do apples grow on trees?

Really well, considering they've been eaten since prehistoric times—that's even before your grandparents were alive. You may have even chomped on an apple that came from the same tree from which your grandparents pulled one. That's because apple trees can bear fruit for as long as 100 years. Seeds grow in the belly of a pollinated flower. That means that a bee took pollen from one flower and gave it to another. The belly and other parts of the flower form an apple. Now the apple can go in *your* belly.

How do volcanoes erupt?

Scorching-ly.

But there's a method to this madness. Volcanoes erupt because of magma, molten rock below the ground. The magma forms 30 to 120 miles (50 to 200 kilometers) beneath Earth's surface. As the magma rises up, the pressure inside the volcano increases. When the pressure is too much to contain, the volcano erupts. You may think the magma is super excited to see our world, but it rises for a different reason: it's less dense than surrounding rock.

Magma

Why do we have hair?

For protection.

And you may be thinking, "C'mon. Hair? How much can *that* protect me?" The answer: a lot! Rather than protect you from arrows or spitballs, it protects you from dust, insects, and other matter. These pesky particles try to enter your body through your eyes, ears, and nose. Eyebrows decrease the amount of light reflected into the eyes.

Why does a ball bounce?

Because it's reaaaaaally excited to see you!

If you toss it to the ground, it wants to come right back to play. And also, physics. *Physics* is the science of matter and how it moves. You apply *force* (a push or pull) to a ball when you send it flying toward the ground. The ground then applies a force back onto the ball, sending it back up again.

World Book, Inc.
180 North LaSalle Street
Suite 900
Chicago, Illinois 60601
USA

For information about other "Answer Me This, World Book" titles, as well as other World Book print and digital publications, please go to www.worldbook.com.

For information about other World Book publications, call 1-800-WORLDBK (967-5325).

For information about sales to schools and libraries, call 1-800-975-3250 (United States) or 1-800-837-5365 (Canada).

Library of Congress Cataloging-in-Publication Data for this volume has been applied for.

Answer Me This, World Book
ISBN: 978-0-7166-3821-6 (set, hc.)

If the world is round, then why is the ground flat?
World Book answers your questions about science
ISBN: 978-0-7166-3827-8 (hc.)

Also available as:
ISBN: 978-0-7166-3837-7 (e-book)

Printed in China by RR Donnelley,
Guangdong Province
1st printing July 2019

Acknowledgments

Cover © Eakkaluktemwanich/Shutterstock; © Ghrzuzudu/Shutterstock
3-69   © Shutterstock
70-71   NOAA Library Collection
72-95   © Shutterstock

Staff

Editorial

Writers
Madeline King
Grace Guibert

Manager, New Content Development
Jeff De La Rosa

Manager, New Product Development
Nick Kilzer

Proofreader
Nathalie Strassheim

Manager, Contracts and Compliance
(Rights and Permissions)
Loranne K. Shields

Manager, Indexing Services
David Pofelski

Digital

Director, Digital Product
Development
Erika Meller

Digital Product Manager
Jonathan Wills

Graphics and Design

Senior Visual
Communications Designer
Melanie Bender

Media Editor
Rosalia Bledsoe

Manufacturing/Production

Manufacturing Manager
Anne Fritzinger

Production Specialist
Curley Hunter